# The Writings of an Old Virginia Country Boy

.

# The Writings of an Old Virginia Country Boy

by

## J. Richard Grove

ISBN: 0-75960-087-2

Library of Congress Control Number 00-093277


This book is printed on acid free paper.

1stBooks - rev. 1/31/01

I dedicate this book to my wife Ditha and our four children:

Mark

Craig

Karen

Elisabeth "Sissy" (11 Feb 64 – 10 Jan 82)

I further dedicate this book to all those people who wanted to write a book but just never got around to it.

# Contents

# Only the Heart Knows Why

At the beginning of the twentieth century in the valley of Virginia, life was a lot different than today. All farms had a flock of chickens, several milk cows, and four or five fat hogs that were butchered every year during cold weather. Farms had fields of corn which were cut in late summer and made into shock. Between the corn shocks the farmer planted a grain, usually wheat. Men came from North Carolina and Tennessee to pick the apples for three cents a bushel. The apple pickers would bed down in one of the farm buildings and return home at the end of the apple season.

Jim and Kitty were born at this time on adjoining farms in the valley. Their families attended the same church, and children of both families attended the same school. They were childhood sweethearts from the beginning. Kitty was born beautiful and with an infectious smile. As she grew older and became aware of the power she had over men, she took advantage of every opportunity. Jim, on the other hand, was nice looking but not handsome. He was a good, kind man and never had a harsh word to say about anyone and was always willing to lend a helping hand.

1

In their early twenties, Jim and Kitty married. Their marriage went well for a while, until Jim found Kitty in the arms of another man. She never missed an opportunity to have a fling if she thought no one else was the wiser. Jim's pleas were never taken seriously. There was the iceman, carpenter, and a dozen others over the years. Kitty's wandering ways ate on poor Jim's mind.

One day after more than twenty years of marriage, Jim for the first time did not come home from work at the usual time. At ten o'clock in the evening, Jim still had not come home. At midnight Kitty called her neighbors thinking for sure that something must have happened to Jim for he did not come home. They looked everywhere for Jim. Finally, someone asked if anyone had looked in the house nearby under construction. So two of the neighbors took a five-cell flashlight and went looking for Jim. As they approached the house under construction – now with a roof on it but the sides still open – they saw a movement. As they got closer, they shined the light on the movement to discover that poor Jim's body was swinging in the wind tied to a rafter.

At Jim's funeral service the family minister Reverend Hall said that God does not want the annihilation of the wicked and that Jesus has conquered death and assured us of every lasting life.

Several months after Jim's death, neighbors noted a change in Kitty's behavior. She no longer showed an active interest in men. She came to realize what a jewel she had had in Jim. She missed him terribly – only to realize it was too late.

In the barnyard behind her house she gathered stalks of nightshade plants and pods from the gypsum weed – both plants have been used since early times to commit suicide. She then took the tool she used to tenderize meat and beat both plants to a pulp. She put the pulp in her dishpan and added a quart of hot water and let it steep overnight. In the morning she drank as much as she could.

Late the next day a neighbor came by Jim's and Kitty's house to borrow a cup of sugar. As the neighbor walked up the steps she heard the dog on the inside of the screen door making an awful chill sounding noise.

She yelled out, "Kitty." As she opened the screen door, she saw Kitty lying on the floor dead.

At Kitty's funeral service, Reverend Hall, like at Jim's service, performed a beautiful sermon. His last words were, "Only the heart knows why."

*J. Richard Grove*

# A Time to Kill

Mr. and Mrs. Pelham-Marshall and their two daughters, Pam and Ruth, often refer to their large Orange County, Virginia, farm, Farnham Park, as home to the wind, for it is located at the head of a narrow valley where the wind seems to never cease. The Pelham-Marshalls are English and spend their off London social season at Farnham Park. Here they are at rest and frequently spend their afternoon with neighbors during the cocktail hour.

Avery Brown and wife and their two daughters from southwest Virginia picked up their meager belongings and moved to one of the tenant houses at Farnham Park where Mr. Brown became farm manager. The Brown's sixteen-year-old son, Buck, an exceptionally handsome young boy is to girls what nectar is to bees. Everywhere the Brown's go with Buck, they are told what a handsome son they have. The Pelham-Marshall daughters are not blind to this fact. And their parents keep a close watch on their daughters, for their inbred English class distinction would not permit otherwise.

Buck helps his dad on the farm; and during the summer's warm weather, Buck works with his shirt off. The Pelham-Marshall girls have been seen stealing a peek at him every chance they get and have been talking and laughing with him when they know that they are safe from their parents' watchful eyes.

Pam, the eldest of the two daughters, is beautiful. Poor Ruth is so-so. Both girls are nice, well-bred young ladies.

In the early forties, farms were still farmed with draft horses and farm work was done mostly by back-breaking labor. By performing the hard physical work demanded of farmers, Buck's body took on the look of a Greek god.

Pam and Buck, now both eighteen, were seeing each other regularly, and Mr. and Mrs. Pelham-Marshall know they cannot do a thing about it. Both daughters are the only children on both sides of their families and when a relative died, their daughters inherited a large part or all of the estate.

Buck registered for the military draft on his eighteenth birthday, and shortly before being sent to Europe, he and Pam were married with the reserved blessing of her parents.

After having completed infantry training, Buck was sent with his unit to North Africa. After U.S. and British forces had done Rommel in, they invaded southern Italy. After Rome fell, Buck's unit once again had Rest and Recuperation leave.

While sitting in an outdoor café overlooking the waterfront, Buck decided married life wasn't for him. He just couldn't leave the girls alone, and they all made it so easy for him. His army buddies jokingly say that he has had every woman from Fort Meade (where they took basic training) to Rome.

For the next few days he frequents the same café. While sipping wine and playing with the girls, he met three elderly Mafia men who were deported from the States before the war. Buck and the men immediately took a liking to each other. After they were acquainted for several days, Buck asked one of them what is the safest way to do one in. He was told "make it look like an accident; if you use a gun, right away it arouses suspicion." "Yes," Buck said, "but if it is your wife and she is wealthy, you are not very likely to avoid a lie detector test."

"Ya, that's true," said his friend, "but there is one way to fool the lie detector, and I am one of only a few who know how.

"Well," said Buck and waited for a reply.

"Look," said his friend, "you son of a bitch, I'll tell you; if you tell anyone, I'll come and get you and kill your ass."

"Don't worry, my ass is safe."

"About an hour before you are to be given the test," said his Mafia friend, eat several teaspoons of horseradish."

As Buck and his unit fought on toward the Rhine, he never forgot what his Mafia friend told him about horseradish.

After Buck was demobilized from the Army, he returned to the farm. Right away Pam and his and her families noticed that Buck is not the same person. He is restless and wants variety when it comes to women. The Army and Europe have changed him.

Months went by and Pam now knows for a fact that Buck is seeing other women. She is not too worried because she dearly loves him and knows that as long as she holds the purse strings that he will never leave her. She knows that he enjoys the good life and will never trade it for being just a bloke.

As more months go by, Buck is now putting on a good front. Those who saw a new Buck when he returned from the war are now seeing an old prewar Buck. Pam noticed that he is now giving her his full attention and staying close to home.

Buck did not forget what his Mafia friend told him about horseradish. He has been thinking about all the good times he has been missing and all the fun he could have in Europe if only he had his wife's money and were free. He is planning, scheming, and thinking about his freedom constantly.

Buck awoke the usual time at daybreak, and it suddenly occurred to him that he and Pam are alone on the farm. Her parents and sister are on a Caribbean cruise, and his parents and sisters are visiting relatives back home in southwest Virginia. The farm is now equipped with a John Deer tractor. Both rear wheels have to be taken in when cultivating corn so that the tires will fit between the corn rows. In order to do this, the rear end of the tractor is suspended off the ground and someone is needed to apply and hold a 4 x 4 three-feet long piece of lumber to the tire rim while a second person with a sledgehammer attacks the other end of the 4 x 4. All of this occurred to Buck like a bolt of lightening – this is the day, this is the time. I'll get Pam to hold the 4 x 4 for there is no one else. As Pam was holding the 4 x 4, a dull thud was heard when the sledgehammer hit her head.

As Pam is lying on the ground beside the tractor – her right leg shaking and her body quivering – blood flowing freely from her crushed skull, Buck runs to the house and dials 911. As the paramedics are attending her, Buck is shocked and is pale as a ghost. He has seen many dead people in the war, but it is different when the dead person is your wife.

Weeks later at the enquiry, authorities tell Buck that they believe it was an accident, but your wife's life insurance company won't be satisfied until you take a lie detector test. Buck readily agrees. On his way home he stopped at the grocery store and bought a bottle of horseradish. He passed the test with flying colors.

After his wife's estate was settled and he had received her life insurance money, he flies to Europe from Washington International Airport to Frankfurt, Germany.

After six years, many women, and many bottles of wine, he returned to Farnham Park nearly broke.

He telegrams ahead of his expected arrival and Ruth and Buck's parents meet him at the airport. After pleasantries and many embraces, they board Ruth's Mercedes wagon and head for home on U. S. 29 South. When they arrived at Farnham Park, Buck said that he would like to go to the cementary – a walled-in area about a hundred yards from the house with a mature cypress tree growing in the center. After a few minutes, he asks to be left alone.

Ruth is still single and she lives with her aging parents. Ruth cannot get over just how handsome Buck still is. She and Buck and her parents frequently make the pleasant drive to Little Washington to dine at The Inn, a five-star restaurant and inn.

Buck has learned that Ruth has even more money than Pam had because her money manager has made exceptionally wise investments that have increased her original holdings many times.

Ruth and Buck hit it off well. They are married two years after Buck's return on the front lawn at Farnham Park. Friends from England and families and friends are present. Shortly after the wedding, Buck becomes restless; after all, he has now led a sedate life for nearly three years. He begins to roam.

Mr. Pelham-Marshall sees the same distrustful pattern in Buck now as when he was married to his daughter Pam.

Every year at Franham Park, after Thanksgiving dinner, Mr. Pelham-Marshall has one of the farm hands bring his pack of beagles to the front lawn where the rabbit shoot begins. Mr. Pelham-Marshall, Buck, and friends spread out in a single line and follow the beagles while listening to their music that is beautiful to a rabbit hunter's ears. The beagles went down the hill across the creek and into a corn field with the hunters following.

As Buck was helping his father-in-law, Mr. Pelham-Marshall, climb the fence that separates the pasture from the corn field, Mr. Pelham-Marshall's twelve gauge shotgun discharges and blows the entire forehead of Buck's head off. Everyone comes running when they realize what has happened. It was obvious that Buck was dead. One of the hunters stayed with Buck while the other went to the house to call the authorities. He had trouble keeping the hounds from Buck. He took his shooting jacket off and placed it over Buck's head. The beagles then wandered off.

The authorities came and took Buck's body. At the funeral he was buried alongside Pam, his first wife.

Mr. Pelham-Marshall's prominent shooting friends, a judge and a U.S. Senator, assured the commonwealth attorney that Buck's death was an accident.

Was it really an accident or was it murder?

# Warminster Plantation

Unlike New England early settlers, Virginia early settlers were born into the English landed gentry. Among these families were the Lees, the Carters, the Byrds, the Fairfaxes, as well as lesser known English noble families. They received thousands of acres of crown land grants along the rivers emptying into the Chesapeake Bay: the James, the Rappahannock, the York, and the Potomac.

Among these families there was a family by the name of Bright. The Bright family seat in their mother country was Warminister Hall, a twenty-two thousand acres estate lying mostly between Warminister and Westbury in Wiltshire in the south of England. Warminster Hall has been in the Bright family for more than five hundred years.

The second eldest son of Brigadier Carter Lee Bright set sail in 1687 from Torbay on HMS Monarch for the Jamestown colony, with his family's blessing and ten thousand English pounds. A letter from King James II to Governor Francis Howard, then governor of the Colony of Virginia, accompanied the Brigadier's son, Colonel Howard Bright. The Brigadier was a favorite hunting companion of the king; and when the king learned

13

that the Brigadier's son Howard was going to live in the Colony of Virginia, he instructed in his letter to the governor that Col. Howard Bright was to be given a twelve-thousand acre crown land grant between the York and the James River.

In addition to the twelve-thousand acres crown grant that he received from the King, Colonel Bright bought an adjoining twenty-two hundred acres consisting of a large, log house, four log slave cabins, and twenty-two men, women, and children slaves, from a Mr. John Taylor, who was returning to England after having lost his wife and three children to typhoid fever.

Among those slaves the colonel chose a man and his wife and their three children to live with him in the large log house until he built his mansion. The remaining slaves lived in the four small log cabins nearby.

Shortly thereafter, Colonel Bright had all the slaves gather under the large live oak tree between the large log house and the cabins. The Colonel told them that he had been in the colony for only a month now but that he had a good feeling about how things work here. He also told them that at Warminster Plantation (his given name for all of his lands) life here will be different from other plantations: there will not be a white overseer; one of you will be the overseer, and that I will be good to you and provide for you. And, in return, I expect the same from you.

Sam, who lived in the large log house with his family and the colonel, was chosen the overseer.

The Colonel left Sam in charge while he went to Jamestown, where he made it known in the two taverns and local businesses that he was going to have a large brick plantation mansion built on his lands and that he would need skilled craftsmen and supplies. They told him that he could hire skilled slave craftsmen from plantation owners and they would know where to get building supplies.

Twelve years later with the help of fourteen craftsmen and laborers, a beautiful four-story, twenty-four room brick mansion with an English cellar stands on a bluff overlooking the York River. The front of the mansion, which faces the river, has sixty steps leading to a porch that is one third as wide as the entire mansion, while the back of the mansion has a full-length porch. Under this porch are steps leading into the English cellar. The cellar has a center aisle with rooms on both sides, and one large room at the far end the width of the cellar, which is the kitchen. House slaves sleep in these cellar rooms. All floors above the cellar have center halls the whole width of the mansion with rooms on both sides. There are rows of dormers on both the front and back roofs. All plantation buildings are also made of bricks that were kilned on the plantation: smokehouse, barns, stables, spring house, hahas, necessities, walks. The old slave cabins are torn down and the new ones are also made of bricks. Warminster Plantation to this day is one of the finest plantations in the South.

Over the three hundred years since the founding of Warminster Plantation, it has reduced by sales and inheritance until today it comprises just over three hundred acres.

The present owners and occupants of the plantation are Colonel Howard Bright and his daughter Lucy, a many generation descent of the first Colonel Bright.

There is one more person who lives in the mansion with the colonel and Miss Lucy – Mama, black Mama, black as the ace of spades, almost two hundred pounds, five feet two inches, bottom broad as an ax handle, broad flat nose, full lips, protruding eyes, short kinky hair, laughs freely. Her roots, too, go back to the beginning of Warminster Plantation. She is a direct descendant of Sam, the plantation's first overseer. Mama cooks for the colonel and Miss Lucy and their guests. If cooks were rated on a ten scale, Mama would be a ten. The kitchen is her domain. Even the colonel and Miss Lucky stay out of her way while in her kitchen. She expects everyone, but the Colonel and

Miss Lucy, to knock on her kitchen door before entering and then wait until they are invited in before entering.

A friend of Mama is a young, Harvard PhD graduate, a light-complexioned, African American, from the adjoining plantation, Lookaway. His name is John D. Skilpot, Jr. He was reared in Harlem by well-educated, affluent parents. His father is an investment broker and a wealthy land investor, and his deceased mother was an associate English Professor at Boston College. Their only son, known to everyone as Skilly, was their only child and was the benefactor of his mother's $200,000 life insurance policy.

Since graduation and his mother's death, Skilly spends most of his time with his now retired friend, former Harvard English professor, Professor Duke, on the professor's Virginia estate, Lookaway Plantation, which joins Warminster Plantation.

Skilly feels and is an equal amoung Professor Duke and his intellectual guests and friends at Lookaway. He often ferries guests to and from Byrd Airport, and he assists the professor in entertaining friends by mixing drinks, and his clever and interesting tales of Harlem and Harvard keeps everyone in a jolly mood.

Skilly met Mama when he had his car, an Italian sports cars import, parked at the village post office. As he returned to his car after having been in the post office, he saw this short, extra stout black woman taking a close look at his car – it was Mama. They immediately found each other fascinating. Mama had never seen a car like this one. Skilly introduced himself and told her that he was a guest at Lookaway. Mama was overwhelmed with this young black man. Never before had she seen anyone so polished and with such a grand manner, especially a black man. Skilly found Mama just as fascinating but for entirely different reasons. Mama talked and looked like Skilly imagined an old fashioned Negro of slavery looked. They were from opposite ends of the spectrum. Mama told Skilly that she lives at Warminster Plantation and asked Skilly to visit her.

Weeks later upon returning from Byrd Airport where Skilly had delivered Professor Duke's guests, he decided to stop at Warminster Plantation to see Mama. Coming up the long tree-lined driveway at Warminster Plantation, Skilly saw three people on the broad lawn in front of this magnificent, grand, old colonial house with its splendid English boxwood gardens. Mama right away recognized Skilly's car and told the Colonel and Miss Lucy that here comes the nice young man who is visiting at Lookaway that I told you about. Mama introduced Skilly to the Colonel and his daughter, Miss Lucy. Skilly made a courtly bow to them and offered them his friendly smile. Right away they took a liking to this polished young man.

After the introduction and an exchange of a few friendly words, Mama said to Skilly, "Come with me to my kitchen. I would like for you to taste the souse I made yesterday." Skilly asked the Colonel and Miss Lucy to be excused and followed Mama. Mama cut a large piece of souse and chopped a small onion fine and sprinkled it over the souse and added a teaspoon of vinegar; this was accompanied with an ample piece of cracklin' cornbread. Skilly told Mama that he had never eaten souse before and it is different and it's good.

While Skilly was eating, he told Mama all about Lookaway Plantation and Professor Duke and his guests, and that he had just come from Byrd Airport after having delivered two guests.

On the way to the airport, the guest sitting in the front seat turned the radio on, Skilly told Mama, and after a few minutes turned the radio off and asked why the state of Virginia has so many religious fanatics.

Mama asked, "What is religious fanatics?"

Skilly told Mama that they are people who live, sleep, and eat religion and that they want the same for all of us. And I wouldn't be surprised that if they had a magic wand, that they would use it to dissolve our government and then install their own people.

In the meantime the colonel and Miss Lucy have come into Mama's kitchen and are taking everything in Skilly is saying about religion – especially the Colonel.

The Colonel acknowledged to Mama that yes he had heard everything Skilly said about religion that that he too had his doubts.

Mama said, "Colonel I doesn't know why youse feel that way because youse is such a good man."

"Mama, the Colonel said, "a person doesn't have to be religious to be a good person. The jails and prisons are full of religious people. In America, more so than in other industrialized countries, if one is critical of religion, that person is akin to a person in the old USSR who was critical of communism. Both will be ostracized. The creationism vs. evolution controversy is causing us to look stupid among educated people everywhere." Mama doesn't understand this fully but Skilly and Miss Lucy do.

Lucy said, "Daddy, you shouldn't talk like that."

"Lucy," the colonel said, "the Earth is my god. One believes or one doesn't believe; and if one doesn't believe, there isn't anything one can do about it. One cannot lie to one's self."

After Skilly left, the Colonel told Mama that Skilly is a fine, young man.

Weeks later Skilly again stops at Warminster Plantation to visit – not just Mama but the Colonel and especially Miss Lucy, since all three showed anticipation at his return.

On this visit Skilly doesn't see anyone and walks around the house to the kitchen. Mama is running water in the sink and doesn't hear Skilly knocking at the screen door; so he enters and walks over to where Mama is and places his hand on her lower back resting on her ample bottom. Mamma whirls around and snappily says, "Looka here nigger. Youse get your black ass out of my kitchen."

They were both shocked – both were taken by surprise.

Skilly said "Mama, you shouldn't call me nigger, the colonel and Miss Lucy might hear you call me nigger. I only meant to be friendly, for I am so glad to see you again." You could now tell by the expression on Mama's face that she wished the floor would rise up and swallow her.

After Mama calmed herself, she told Skilly that she is baking a cherry pig. Skilly asked, "What is a cherry pig?" Mama told him that it is a rectangular, flattened piece of pie dough about the size of a large pizza and that it is then covered with a layer of tart cherries and sprinkled with nutmeg and brown sugar then it is rolled and baked in my woodstove oven until done.

"Sounds delicious, may I please have a piece when it is done?"

"Yes, you sure can," and later while still hot, she cut a large piece and poured cinnamon milk and sprinkled powdered sugar over it and offered it to Skilly.

Moments later Skilly thanked Mama and said, "I have never tasted anything so delicious."

When Skilly was half done eating, the colonel came into the kitchen and greeted Skilly and said to Mama, "I smelled your cooking and just couldn't resist the temptation."

Mama said, "Sit down, and I fix you right up."

While they were eating the colonel told Skilly that he heard that a European and an American educator were the guests of the professor.

"Yes," Skilly said "and the talks they had were really worth listening to, for instance the German professor said that American educators must be realistic in their goals. Setting a goal for all students to become high school graduates makes about as much sense as your commissioner of baseball setting a goal for all ball players to bat fifty home runs a season. All students, like all ball players, do not have the right stuff – as you Americans like to say. He went on to say that in Europe after completing the seventh grade, students that are academically inclined continued their studies while all other attend trade schools.

Mr. Potts, the American educator, said that we have more teachers today with master's degrees and PhD's than ever before and never before has any country spent so much money to educate their students, and our federal and state governments will spend billions more of our tax dollars on education, and this will not solve the problem. Teachers' salaries could be increased to one hundred thousand dollars, and this too would not solve the problem. Only recently, he continued, a news article stated that even our brightest students do not do as well as the brightest students in other countries. He emphasized by clearing his throat and increasing his voice that our educational system has become a dollar-gobbling monster and a high school and college training ground for professional sports.

Herr Schmidt, the German professor, then brought to everyone's attention that if school attendance is your only requirement for high school graduation, then even a monkey could qualify. Is it not better, he asked, to have a large majority of your students well educated than to have all students' education in doubt? You Americans are going to drown yourselves in democracy.

The Colonel asks Skilly, "What do you think of all this?"

Well Sir, the professors have raised points about education that, as far as I know, have never been addressed before. I, too, have concerns about many different things. For instance, why do so many pop artists find it necessary to act and dress like freaks in order to make music? And why do so many women today sport tatoos and body piercing? And why does our government not legalize drugs and prostitution, bodily pleasures have been with us since the beginning, and neither is going to go away. If people want something bad enough, they will get it one way or another. Didn't anyone, Skilly continued, learn anything from Prohibition? The root of some of our problems may be that our women don't make their men walk the line anymore."

Skilly ended by saying that there are many things wrong with our people, our government, and our country, but where is there a better people, a better government, and a better country?

The Colonel told Skilly that he hit the nail on the head. Mama and Miss Lucy applauded.

The very next day Miss Lucy telephoned Lookaway and asked to speak to Skilly. She asked Skilly to please come right away. Skilly told Professor Duke about the telephone call and that Miss Lucy did not sound like herself – something dreadful must have happened.

The professor told Skilly to go on; and if I am needed, please don't hesitate to call me.

As Skilly arrived at Warminister Plantation, a nurse was leaving. Skilly thought to himself, it couldn't be Miss Lucy, so it must be Mama or the Colonel.

A number of cars were parked in the parking lot and on the lawn. The three family dogs, a bluetick and two labs, were making awful wolf-like howls. Skilly slowly open the front door and was greeted by two cairns. He still didn't see anyone and proceded on to the back of the house there in the kitchen and the adjoining library were the mourners.

When Miss Lucy saw Skilly, she took aholt of his arm and told him that the Colonel died (she always referred to her dad as Colonel). And his last words were "please call Skilly." He was buried at

Arlington National Cemetery with full military honors.

Miss Lucy and Skilly became close friends and after a six months courtship, they married. Skilly moved in with his wife, and Mama was so glad to be part of this new family.

Lucy (everyone was calling her Lucy now) and Skilly discovered when the Colonel's will was read, that the Colonel was deeply in debt. Skilly assured his wife that she shouldn't worry since his inheritance would more that take care of everything. Mama lived to see and hear the patter of little feet. And for the first time in more than three hundred years, black blood flowed in the veins of Warminster Plantation's descendants.

# A Stillness in the Land

The day Sissy died there was a stillness in the land. It was as though a supreme force had called for complete quietness and no movement.

The two Dobermans at Sissy's house did not eat their feed. There were no birds at the feeders. The prevailing west breeze on her front porch was not there. The tractor trailers climbing the Blue Ridge Mountains going west could no longer be heard. There was a stillness in the land.

The Angus cattle did not call their calves to nurse. Nursing calves were not heard calling their mothers. The usual hound was not heard chasing a fox on Allen Mountain. There was a stillness in the land.

The rooster did not crow this morning. The dogs lazed about and showed no interest in making their daily rounds. All during the day the leaves were perfectly still. The few clouds that were in the sky showed no movement. There was a stillness in the land.

Late that night a Virginia state trooper knocked at their door and informed her family that their daughter, Sissy, was killed in an automobile accident. As the trooper was returning to his patrol car, a strong wind rose from the east and a cow was heard calling her calf. The stillness was broken. It was gone.

# Sissy

I miss you
I miss seeing you primp
I miss seeing you do your homework
I miss seeing you cuddle a puppy


I listen for your happiness
I listen for your giggle
I listen for your laughter
I listen for your voice in the lonely wind


I miss your giggle
I miss your laughter
I miss your smiles
I miss you calling me Daddy
I miss the promise that was yours


I look for your face when I see young girls
I look for your face when I see passing clouds


I remember your voice in the school play
I remember the poetry you wrote

*J. Richard Grove*

I remember how bright you were
I remember your maturity for someone so young


I think about you all the time

Daddy




Written by the author in memory of his daughter, Elisabeth "Sissy" Ann Grove, 11 Feb. 1964 – 10 Jan. 1982.

# Sweet Lucy

In downtown Richmond, Virginia, in July 1946, it was almost all white. Only occasionally was a black person seen. Crime was rare and murder was almost unknown. Streetcars were the mode of public transportation and not noisy, stinking buses that are used today. This was a time when blacks were politely referred to as Negroes, and they were treated as inferior. They had their own eating, sleeping, and social places – regardless of character and intellect.

While working part time at the sundries counter in the Broad Street Standard Drug Store, selling mostly apple, cherry, and peach wines for forty-nine cents a bottle, to mostly winos and others who enjoyed wine but couldn't afford better quality, I learned that blacks have their own names for each wine. I have forgotten their names for apple and cherry, but I will never forget, because of a beautiful black woman, that when they wanted peach wine they always asked for Sweet Lucy. There never seemed to be a scarcity of black customers for Sweet Lucy. Where they came from, I don't know.

About my third day at work this most beautiful black woman, about twenty years old, with full bust and buttocks, and tastefully dressed and well groomed and with a walk that would put a double whammy on all real men, stopped about five feet from where I was working. Our eyes locked. For a few brief moments, we seemed to be in a trance. We were embarrassed and uncomfortable. We knew that there was something there. When she finally spoke, she asked for Sweet Lucy. By this time, I knew what Sweet Lucy was. I put the bottle of peach wine in a bag and handed it to her. She was out of sight before I realized she hadn't paid for the wine. About ten minutes later she returned and paid. Again there was this something between us.

During the next two years that I worked there, she came two or three times a week for Sweet Lucy. By this time I was calling her Sweet Lucy. If I were busy, she always waited until I was free and she never failed to give me one of her big beautiful smiles.

Today it would not be a problem, but in those days blacks and whites did not socialize together.

During those two years her life style began to tell on her – too much wine and lax grooming; and, who knows, maybe her man was rough on her – although in my presence she never came with one.

Today, fifty years later, I sometimes think about Sweet Lucy and hope that things worked out all right for her.

*J. Richard Grove*

# Don't You Cry for Me

At the end of WWII, during the military occupation of Vienna, Austria, by French, British, Russian, and American armed forces, there was an unforgettable young Austrian woman on the scene. She was known by soldiers of the four occupying powers as Muscle Lil. Her favorite were the Americans. They were the ones with the money, the booze, the cars, and carefree ways.

After the Berlin Airlift came to a halt, Sergeant Hoy Yowell from Charlottesville, Virginia, was transferred from Frankfurt, Germany, to Wiesbaden, Germany. Six months later he was transferred to Tulln air Force Base, twenty miles from Vienna in the Russian occupation zone of Austria. Austria, like Germany, was divided into four zones of occupations. Like Berlin, Vienna also was divided into four zones of occupations.

Muscle Lil was a switch hitter; she moved from one of the occupying zones to another with ease. She could not have cared less about military secrets, military functions, and the cold war. She could always be found where the social excitement was.

After only hours at Tulln, Sgt. Yowell heard the name Muscle Lil for the first time of many times thereafter. From Tulln to Vienna, Americans were permitted to travel by train and by the use of one road; no stopping or turning around by Americans was permitted by the Russians.

Across the street from the Tulln/Vienna train station in Vienna was a favorite hangout for American military personnel and also Muscle Lil – Café Wien.

Sgt. Yowell's first trip to Vienna was by train with two G.I.'s from the base. During the twenty mile train ride to Vienna, they told him about Vienna's high culture and its people. When they arrived at the station, they asked him to go with them to Café Wien so that if Muscle Lil were there, he could meet her. As they walked through the door of the café, a young woman got up from a nearby table where three men were seated and walked in front of Sgt. Yowell and stopped. She turned around to face everyone in the café and yelled, "Here's a goddamn, good-looking man." She then hauled off and hit him on his right shoulder so hard that he lost his balance and fell flat across a nearby table. An American soldier sitting at this table with his girlfriend said, "Whatcha trying to do, man?" Everyone roared with laughter. Sgt. Yowell was later told that Muscle Lil was in her usual good form. Upon leaving with her three friends, Muscle Lil came to the table where Sgt. Yowell was sitting and kissed him on the top of his head. Someone in a far corner yelled, "Tell her you love her." She left without saying a word.

When Muscle Lil was at Café Wien, customers stayed longer, drinking good Austrian beer and eating their superb sausages, while listening to Lil's philosophy on just about every subject under the sun. She was a conversationalist of the first rank. This resulted in a large increase in business for Herr Schmitz, the proprietor, so he always picked up her tab. She never seemed to have money anyway. Lil wasn't as tough on Hitler as one might expect. She reminded her audience that throughout military history, plunder, massacres, and rapes were common. She reminded the Americans of their ill treatment of Native Americans, and asked, "Is the massacre of one million Indian men, women, and children any less of a crime than Hitler's massacre of ten million?" And after all, whose land was it?" Religion was a subject that always, for some reason, annoyed her. She reminded her listeners that Churchill, Einstein, Shaw, and she named a dozen other big brains of the twentieth century, whose names have since been forgotten, who did not believe in the hereafter. She would then ask those listening that with all the scientific knowledge we have today and the fears of the Dark Ages long gone, how they could still believe. Of course someone would always ask about the Jews and of course Lil always had an answer. Her response would be that for thousands of years and by many nations, the Jew had been persecuted and disliked. Is it not time, she would ask, that they take a good, long, close look at themselves – and ask themselves why? She thought Russian Communism would have been successful if they had spent half of their military rubles on improving their country and let their people have the remaining rubles to improve their standard of living. After all, she would say, no one ever won the hearts and minds of people with guns. They could have made Russia a showplace. The world today might have been an altogether different world if they had taken this road.

The occupying powers rotated military control of Vienna on a monthly basis. At Allied Military Headquarters, at the end of each month, the outgoing occupying power's flag was lowered and the incoming power's flag was raised. Each did his best in displaying military smartness, when parading troops from barracks to Allied Military Headquarters preceding the Allied agreed upon ceremony.

The Russians were always impressive. When it was their turn to take control of the city, their well uniformed troops smartly marched from the Russian barracks to Allied Military Headquarters, while singing beautiful Russian marching songs. Those who heard them singing will never forget.

The Russian commandant of all Soviet armed forces in Austria always led the Russian forces from the back seat of a chauffeur-driven command staff vehicle. Lord behold – sitting beside the commandant in the December 1950 changeover was none other than Muscle Lil. Sgt. Yowell was quoted as having said that of all that he had read and of all the talk he had heard of this incident since, no one can recall of a similar incident. Some said that Muscle Lil forced her way into the vehicle while it was in motion and that the commandant did not evict her because he thought it would be better to let things be rather than make a public scene. Others said that they both had been drinking vodka, while others said that Muscle Lil threatened to expose the commandant's love-making if he did not cooperate. Anyway, the Austrian press had a field day. The commandant was relieved of his command and transferred back to Moscow. Muscle Lil would, for reasons known only to herself, never talk about her escapade. She wouldn't even drink to it.

Sgt. Yowell was a twenty-five year old air force sergeant with a new Opel Olympia automobile and with plenty of money. One could drive for miles and miles in Europe and not see another automobile that was not owned by an American. The Austrians, as well as troops of the other occupying forces, were very, very poor in comparison. Needless to say, those of the American military forces were one heck-of-a-force for the European ladies to reckon with. Sgt. Yowell, an old Virginia country boy, never even dreamed that he would ever have it nearly so good.

One evening he was dancing with a fraulein in a Ring Strasse café to "My Blue Heaven" when in walked a Russian major and a captain with their Austrian girl friends. Both officers were badly in need of a shave and were absent without leave. After everyone had danced for awhile, one of their girl friends – Muscle Lil – came to Sgt. Yowell and said that they did not want to fight. The Russians and their girlfriends shook hands with Sgt. Yowell and exchanged cigarettes. Lil gave the impression that the Russians had been educated to believe that fighting was one of the two most favorite things that Americans love to do. This was Sgt. Yowell's only social contact with the Russians. Shortly thereafter, upon completion of his overseas tours, he was rotated back to the States.

While Sgt. Yowell was standing on the Tarmac with a rotation group waiting for their plane to be brought to loading position, Muscle Lil arrived with tears in her eyes to say good-bye. An army colonel, who was a doctor in the medical corp, left the group and walked over to where Lil stood. He kissed her on the forehead and they embraced. They said a few words to each other and he then brought her to the waiting group. In unison, they said, "We'll miss you Lil." She said, "Ja, I'll miss you bastards too." As they were boarding, she yelled to Sgt. Yowell, "I'll miss you, old good-looking. Don't you cry for me."

After they were airborne, the colonel said that he knew Lil's family before the war and that she was from an old noble Hungarian family – the Mihalyi's. The letter "I" on the end of a Hungarian family name denotes nobility. Soon after Hitler occupied Austria, he instructed that the "I" be dropped. Lil's father was Baron Frans Joseph von Mihalyi, who served as a surgeon general in the Austrian-Hungarian army during the first World War. He was killed just outside Vienna in a bunker while commanding German troops defending Vienna from the advancing Russians in 1945. Lil, the colonel went on to say, was one of three

Mihalyi children. All three graduated from the University of Vienna with honors. The two sons went on to pursue medical degrees from the University of Heidelberg as did their father, grandfathers, and great grandfather. Lil obtained a Ph.D. from the University of Vienna.

The colonel met the baron, Lil's father, while attending a medical conference at the University of Heidelberg shortly before WWII and was invited by the baron to accompany him to the Austrian/Hungarian boarder to spend a weekend at the family's baronial estate: Schloss Magyarovar.

Although they were on their way home, tears and choked voices said that it was a sad day for most of them.

In 1995, almost fifty years later, Hoy Yowell and his wife visited his wife's Viennese relatives. While sitting in the living room watching German television, he thought about long, long ago – the good times, Café Wien, and Muscle Lil. Why not, he asked himself, check out Café Wien, see if it is still there? He told his wife what he was up to. She gave him a big kiss and told him to watch out for Muscle Lil.

# The Last Love Letter

Dear Ruthie,

I received your letter today.

It has been more than sixty years since I brought Bob, my college roommate, home for the weekend. You being so beautiful, it was no wonder that he would fall in love with you. After all, I feel that even Marilyn would have been conscious of your beauty in her presence. And of course you did what your heart told you to do. I guess the song "Tennessee Waltz" was written especially for me. At home in the privacy of my room I cried like a baby. I know men aren't supposed to cry, but I did. But it didn't do any good, for the hurt and loneliness was still there. And wherever I went for all these years, it was always with me. I know that those who have been hurt get over it and move on, but for me it was not to be.

I obtained a graduate degree in structural engineering – specializing in stress structural. After having written many articles on the subject that were published in the leading engineering publication and my performance, I became the most sought after engineer in my field. Before I retired several years ago, I was commanding a consulting fee of fifty thousand dollars. I know this sounds like a lot of money for a few hours of my time, but my advice usually resulted in several or more million dollars in savings for my clients. After all it was a small price to pay. My work took me to five continents, and I almost always checked out those structures that were built long ago – especially the cathedrals built in the 12th and 13th century in Europe.

I know that you are very much alive, but with a husband that abused you both physically and mentally – at least a small part of you must have died – so when I entered those great temples of God, I always lit a candle for you. You see – you were always with me. Yes, I've had many love affairs – even been proposed to a couple of times. But my longing for you always won out in the end.

My sister who taught your two children kept me informed of the local news, including news of you and your family.

After all these years, until lately, I often thought of the wonderful times we could have had together. Today I am like the expert swimmer who drowned six feet from shore. Sure, everyone said that if they had been that swimmer they would have swam that six feet. But the swimmer was exhausted – there was no more energy. It was all gone. There was nothing left.

If only you had written a month ago, maybe even only a week ago.

Richard

*J. Richard Grove*

# Tell the Story about the Chicken

For Sunday dinner, before WWII, the farmer's wife would choose a chicken from the barnyard flock. After throwing a handful of shell corn on the ground and grabbing the unlucky chicken, the farmer's wife would place its head on a chopping block; and with one swing of the hatchet or ax, the chicken's head would drop to the ground. The released headless chicken would, for a few seconds, run like crazy all over the barnyard.

<u>But no chicken has ever shown any movement after having been in the frying pan.</u>

If in the future someone tells you about an outside of the body experience or having seen beautiful lights at the end of a tunnel, you tell that someone the story about the chicken.

*J. Richard Grove*

# Pick Six

In September 1998, Bill Will and Mrs. Will drove to Madison, Wisconsin, so that Mrs. Will could attend a porcelain repair class given by the University of Wisconsin. The class fees included room and board for the two of them at the University.

While she attended class, Bill would while away time walking the streets looking in antique shops and anything that caught his interest – like the famous Houdini Escape Artist Museum.

The first day they were there, Bill purchased a Big Game Lottery ticket. Wisconsin participates in an eleven state super lottery. The lottery for this drawing was estimated to be worth $267,000,000 and except for a lottery in Spain during the previous year, this amount was the world's largest. He bought his lottery ticket from a small shop on Luck Street run by a dark complexioned clerk from India. After exchanging a few pleasantries with the clerk, Bill told him if he won he would buy a round trip ticket to India so that he could see his family.

Three days later it was announced on the local radio station as well on national TV news by all three major networks that one ticket sold in

Madison, Wisconsin, matched all six numbers and that after taxes the lucky ticket holder would walk away with $187,000,000. The International World News Network picked up on this winning and now people of the world knew that one of them is now $187,000,000 richer.

The day following the winning ticket announcement, while reading the morning newspaper, during breakfast, Bill Will remembered that he had purchased a lottery ticket. He removed his lottery ticket form his wallet and turned to page two of the newspaper for the lottery results.

His lottery ticket matched the winning lottery ticket numbers.

He returned his lottery ticket to his wallet and right there in the dining room, while having breakfast with his wife and dozens of other people, he vomited. He refused to let anyone call 911 and assured everyone that after a few minutes of rest, he would be all right. His wife and a dining room attendant cleaned up the mess, while Bill gathered his wits. Bill's wife asked him, "What is wrong with you?" After he told her about his winning the lottery, she almost fainted. They left the dining room supporting each other.

When Bill and his wife returned to their room, Bill telephoned the Madison Chief of Police and informed him that he held the winning lottery ticket number and asked if one of his officers could escort him and his wife to collect the winnings. A few minutes later, the chief of police and one of his officers arrived in the police chief's cruiser.

At the lottery office, after having qualified Bill's winning lottery number and lottery ticket, everyone congratulated Bill and his wife. He was presented a cashier's check for $187,000,000. Bill thanked everyone. The chief asked Bill if there is anything else we can do for you. Bill said, "Yes, will you please take us to a bank so that we may deposit this check?" After Bill deposited the check, the chief and his officer returned Bill and his wife to their University of Wisconsin dormitory room.

While Bill's wife attended the two remaining days of porcelain class and after talking it over with his wife, Bill had his Wisconsin bank wire $150,000,000 to the Richmond, Virginia, Federal Reserve Bank for deposit at 6.7% interest – a return of more than ten million dollars a year before taxes for 30 years.

Before returning home to Roanoke, Virginia, Bill wrote a thank you letter to the chief of police and enclosed a check for $25,000 to benefit the Madison, Wisconsin, police department. Bill then walked to the small shop on Luck Street where he purchased his lucky lottery ticket. As soon as Bill entered the store, the clerk from India said as soon as he saw Bill, "You are the one." Bill nodded his head. He then wrote a check for $25,000 dollars and gave it to the Indian. When he saw the amount of the check, he gave Bill a big bear hug and cried like a baby.

Bill and his wife returned to Virginia on a chartered jet. They bought a large, old, historical Virginia plantation and a winter home in the U. S. Virgin Islands. And what else have they done? Everything their hearts desire.

The Indian bought a one-way airline ticket to India and never returned to America.

The chief of police has retired and spends summer by a lake in Minnesota and the winter in Miami, Florida.

# Everyone Called Her Pussy

Between the two great wars, in the east end of Richmond, Virginia, lived a family by the name of Schwartz. They were a lower, working class family. Mr. Schwartz was a janitor for one of the tobacco companies. And his wife stayed home and took care of their five children, four sons and a daughter. Their home was dilapidated and poorly managed. And although they had electricity, there was no plumbing. All houses and families in the immediate area were similar. Both parents were uneducated and their social graces were nonexistent. They both were born and grew up here, as did their parents.

Peggy, their daughter, was the youngest of the five children. When she was three years old, nearly four, her father brought a stray kitten home that he found wandering the streets while he walked home from work. Right away Peggy took a liking to the kitten. It wasn't long before they were inseparable. Like Mary's little lamb, everywhere Peggy went the kitten was sure to follow. When they became separated, Peggy would ask everyone, "Where is my pussycat?" If no one at home knew where the kitten was, she would go out on the street and ask neighbors and strangers, "Where is my pussycat?"

It wasn't long before family members started to call Peggy Pussy. Neighbors too started to call her Pussy as well. Now everyone who knew Peggy was calling her Pussy. As she grew older and went out into the world, the nickname followed her. For as long as she lived and wherever she went she was always called Pussy.

As Pussy grew older she began to observe and study people and ask herself questions. She noticed that all people do not dress alike, do not talk alike, do not live the same lifestyles. In her early teens she noticed that some people eat more gracefully than others. She noticed that these people palmed their knife and fork and used their forefinger for leverage when cutting food, while her kind held their fork in a vertical position. These other people did not eat with their elbows or an arm on the table. And that these people put their napkins in their laps rather than leaving them on the table. And that soup was eaten from the side of the spoon, not the end. Pussy was growing up fast and taking everything in. She was different from her family and the ones she knew.

In 1942 during World War II, Pussy was 17 years old and a senior in high school. She now had blossomed into a beautiful young woman; she resembled a young Elizabeth Taylor with black hair and indigo blue eyes. And all body parts were ample and in the right places.

She was friendly to everyone but associated only with those from whom she could learn. Her craving for knowledge to improve herself was forever present. She devoured books that taught self-improvement such as Emily Post's *Etiquette* and *The Personality of a House*, also by Emily Post. She didn't only read these and other self-improvement books, she practically memorized them. Although she still lived at home and in her parents' world, she knew that their world was different and yearned for the world of her friends of choice. She now felt comfortable in their presence and in their homes. Among her girl friends were two early classmates who were now attending finishing school in Switzerland. She especially observed them closely and wasn't bashful about asking questions. Although she was so much more beautiful and her presence was subdued by her as much as possible, she never let it interfere with her friendship. She seldom dated; and when she did, it was always with boys she felt were her own kind.

Upon graduating from high school, Pussy answered a legal secretary classified ad in the *Richmond-Times Dispatch*. When Pussy dialed the help wanted number, the attorney who placed the ad, a Mister Robertson, answered the telephone. He explained to her that during these war times that employers could not make a fastidious choice and that although she felt she might not be qualified that he would like to interview her anyway. An appointment was made for the following day at two in the afternoon. Mister Robertson told Pussy at the end of the interview that he was impressed with the way she handled herself and her dress and her good looks and that he would be delighted if she would start work the following day. She said that she too was delighted and would start work the following day.

Mr. Robertson, her employer, was in his late seventies and he and Mrs. Robertson were childless. When they learned that Peggy's nickname was Pussy, they too called her Pussy. They eventually became so fond of Pussy that they asked her to come and live with them. She enjoyed the company of Mr. and Mrs. Robertson and their beautiful old Colonial brick home with its period antique furniture and their lovely formal gardens. Just about everywhere the Robertsons went, they insisted that Pussy go with them – to their beach house, their farm, and shopping. For the first time in her young life, Pussy now saw how affluent people live who have servants – all their needs are taken care of by devoted help.

The Robertsons now know of Pussy's family background, and they are impressed with her effort to improve herself. They make welcome suggestions, and Pussy is always receptive and grateful.

One 2 May 1945 Mrs. Robertson received a telephone call from California that her only sister had died. Pussy assured Mr. and Mrs. Robertson that she would take care of everything while they were away. Ten days later on their return trip home, the airplane that was bringing the Robertsons' home had an inflight malfunction that caused the plane to crash. There were no survivors.

Never before had Pussy known grief.

A week after the accident, Mr. Marshall, an attorney family friend of the Robertsons and also an acquaintance of Pussy through the Robertsons, called her on the telephone at the Robertson's home and said to Pussy that he would like to see her at four PM in his office. When she arrived at Mr. Marshall's office, he embraced Pussy and told her that we both have lost two dear friends. They both cried in each other's arms. Mr. Marshall went on to tell her that Mr. and Mrs. Robertson had made him the executor to their wills and that she was the sole benefactor. He further told her that she is now a wealthy young lady. And that in addition to their beach house and large farm that there are many hundreds of thousands of dollars invested in stocks and bonds – their total estate is worth in excess of two million dollars.

He walked Pussy to her car and told her that he and Mrs. Marshall would always be available if ever they were needed.

Shortly before Christmas, Pussy's friend who completed finishing school in Switzerland phoned Pussy and asked if she would go with her and two girlfriends to a Christmas party at the officers' club at Byrd Air Force Base near Richmond. Pussy immediately accepted; she was only too glad to get out of the house.

When they entered the officers' club, all eyes were on Pussy – as usual. A lieutenant met them at the door and took their wraps and led them to the punch bowl. While they and the lieutenant were having their drinks, Pussy could not help noticing a handsome serviceman on the other side of the room who kept staring at her. One of the girls asked the lieutenant who that man is who keeps staring at Pussy. The lieutenant told the girls that he is Colonel Longwood and that he is at twenty-three the youngest full colonel or the equivalent in all of our armed forces. And that he is a fighter pilot and flew more combat sorties than anyone in the Air Force during WWII. He went on to say that at the end of the war, he was the commanding officer of the 81st Fighter Wing Station in Germany, comprised of 125 fighter aircraft and 1,200 airmen. The lieutenant then looked at Pussy and said, "What did you say your name is?" Pussy said, "Pussy, Pussy Schwartz." He said, "Uh, how would you girls like to meet the colonel?" Three girls in unison said, "Yes". Pussy did not say anything. The lieutenant went to the colonel and asked him if he would like to meet the girls. As he was being introduced to them, he tried to do the right thing, but he just could not keep his eyes off of Pussy. Pussy was embarrassed and so was the colonel. Pussy asked the colonel if it weren't really something to have been promoted to full colonel at the age of twenty-three? The colonel replied, "Not really. Alexander the Great conquered all the known world at that time when he was only eighteen." The colonel excused himself, and while he was gone, the lieutenant told the girls that the colonel was from an old and wealthy Charleston, South Carolina, family and that they owned coal mines and railroads. Pussy might have been impressed if she had been told this before her inheritance – but not now. She too had means.

All the girls accepted Pussy's invitation to spend the night at her home, for they were anxious to see where she now lives. As they open the front door, the telephone was ringing. The voice on the other end said, "This is Robert Longwood; may I please speak to Miss Schwartz?"

Pussy said, "I didn't expect your call so soon."

"Then you did expect my call?"

"Yes, but..." Pussy left "but" hanging in the air.

The colonel knew that this was the most important mission that he had ever flown. No mission before had ever raised the cold sweat and the possibility of an uncertain failure feeling as this one. The colonel knew by his Southern breeding that this young lady with her soft voice and never saying or doing anything to draw attention to herself was a special lady. Not only was she beautiful and tastefully groomed, but her manners were impeccable. He knew at once that he wanted to marry her.

After Pussy and Robert had several dates, he asked her to marry him. She knew that he loved her and that she loved him, but she did not give an answer.

She telephoned Mr. and Mrs. Marshall and asked if she could see them. The Marshalls invited Pussy for dinner. While they were having before dinner drinks, Pussy told them all about her new friend, the 23 year old Colonel Longwood. Mr. Marshall said, "My God, Pussy, are you sure he is only 23? I was 50 when I was promoted to Colonel in the army reserve. Most regular peace time officers with 30 years service never make colonel. In spite of what the preachers say, you only get one shot at life – so make it a good one. Marry your colonel."

On Pussy's next date with Robert, she asked him, "Will you marry me?" He took her in his arms and gave her a long kiss. He did not answer her question – there was no need to. They both knew they were madly in love with each other.

Pussy took Robert to meet her parents at the new house that she bought them out of her inheritance. It was in a much nicer area of Richmond. Although Robert did not let on, he was amazed that someone as polished and fashionable as Pussy came from this family. They were good people but not nice people. He did not care; he was in love, and he was not a dyed-in-the-wool snob.

Like many planters' sons from the Old South, Robert attended the University of Virginia, Mr. Jefferson's school. After completing one year, he enlisted in the Army Air Corps. He and Pussy were married in the University of Virginia chapel under crossed swords of the Reserve Officers Training Corps cadets. Robert's friends and family members from South Carolina were present, as well as Pussy's friends and family from Richmond.

Pussy sold her inherited Virginia properties, and she and her husband took up residence on

Robert's twelve-thousand acre South Carolina Longwood Plantation that he inherited from his grandfather on his twenty-first birthday.

They spent the rest of their lives when not holding hands, hunting, shooting, fishing, and sailing with their wealthy friends who owned or leased shooting and fishing lodges on four continents. In between times they usually rode to the hounds either in Virginia or England. They and their friends owned second and sometimes third homes in the Caribbean, the South of France, and Switzerland, as well as homes in the Hamptons and principle cities of Europe, North and South America. They lived this life style all their married life.

Pussy died a natural death at age 73 while spending some time at their South Carolina home, Longwood Plantation. She was buried in the Longwood Cementary on the plantation. Pussy and Robert when home at Longwood always had before dinner drinks in the library. Now that Robert was alone, he continued to have before dinner drinks as before.

Shortly after Pussy died, George, the butler, brought Mr. Robert his daily before dinner drink only to discover that Mr. Robert was fast asleep sitting up in a comfortable wing chair. Several times he brought his drink only to discover to his surprise that he was still asleep. The next time George placed his hand on Mr. Robert's shoulder, only then did George realize that Mr. Robert was dead. He was buried alongside his beloved wife, Pussy.

Those who knew him best said that he died because he lacked the will to live without his beloved Pussy.

*J. Richard Grove*

# Pig Tail Company

John P. McGahey of McGaheyville, Virginia, was born 3 May 1925. McGaheyville was named after his grandfather, who was the most prominent and successful farmer in the area at the time. John P. was named after his grandfather. The McGaheys were handsome and very agile farm people. John P., as he was called respectfully by everyone, was no exception. He, like his father and grandfather before him, excelled at everything. All through his years at McGaheyville High School, he was the school's most outstanding athlete and he was no slacker in his studies. Upon returning home from his first day at school, they asked him how he liked school. He said, "It was all right, but I don't think I'll go back." From the sixth through the twelfth grades he ran a trap line during the winter months. The first year he trapped he caught two mice in one trap setting. When he told his mom and dad, they laughed their fool heads off. It took him a long time to figure out why they thought it was so funny. Because of his good looks and winning ways, throughout elementary and high school he always had the prettiest girlfriend. He was an only child.

On 31 December 1943, he was inducted into the U.S. Army. After he and 219 other Virginians were outfitted in army gear at Ft. Meade, Maryland, three days later they were shipped by troop train to Jacksonville, Florida. From there they were transported by army convoy to Camp Gordon Johnson, Florida, about 55 miles southwest of Tallahassee.

John P. and his fellow Virginians were assigned to Infantry "A" Company 4th Bn 8th Regiment of the 4th Army. This was it! Life would never be the same again for the next three and a half years.

During a late evening training skirmish, a jeep Pvt. McGahey was riding in hit and killed a wild sow. Six of her piglets ran off into the palmetto thickets. The seventh one didn't move and it squealed beside its dead mother with all its might. The soldiers thought it was very funny, but John P. thought otherwise. He jumped out of the jeep, picked up the squealing young piglet, and made calm, soothing sounds to it. From that day on, John P. and his comrades and that piglet were the best of friends. They called it Squealer.

Three months later, Pvt. McGahey and his outfit were told to be ready to be shipped overseas. By this time, Squealer was almost like a member of the company. They couldn't decide what to do with Squealer. They knew that Squealer would have to remain behind. Pvt. McGahey hit upon the idea to cut Squealer's tail off and take it with him for good luck. This he did. That evening upon leaving the mess hall there was one salt shaker with no salt in it. John P. used the salt to preserve Squealer's tail. Salted down for three weeks and wrapped in a handkerchief, it was as well preserved as any rabbit's foot you ever saw.

"A" Company with Pvt. McGahey and the Virginians landed in Glasgow, Scotland, and then they were shipped to Southern England for more infantry training, while waiting for D-Day. D-Day arrived. Units of the 4th Army were among the first troops to hit the beaches. "A" Company was among them.

By the end of the war in Europe, of the 227 soldiers of "A" Company, 92 were killed. One of the dead, an officer from Winchester, Virginia, was found with a Holy Bible in his left breast pocket. A 30 caliber German Mauser bullet had gone through the bottom right corner into his heart, causing instant death. Written on the inside front cover were these words: "If anything will bring you back alive, this will. Aunt Kitty." Sixty-eight were severely wounded. Sixty-six received minor injuries. Pvt. McGahey was unhurt.

Twelve men of "A" Company carried rabbits' feet for good luck. Three had four leaf clovers.

Twenty-two soldiers carried an assortment of good luck charms. Pvt. McGahey carried a pig's tail. He was the only soldier of "A" Company who survived the war without so much as a scratch.

An historian, while studying D-Day invasion units, discovered the story about the pig tail. He wrote a letter to the present commander of "A" Company informing him of its WWII history. The commander in return sent a copy of the historian's letter, with a companion letter attached, through the military chain of command to the U.S. Army Chief of Staff requesting that "A" Company be designated the Pig Tail Company. Exactly three weeks later "A" Company commander received permission from his immediate superior to so designate the company.

Today "A" Co. 4th Bn 8th Regiment of the 4th U.S. Army, after 50 years is still known as the Pig Tail Company.

It saw action in the Korean War and the Vietnam War. Although casualties were reported during these wars, no deaths were recorded.

Old soldiers of "A" Company give all the good luck credit to the pig tail.

# A Virginia County Strikes It Rich

Madison County, a predominantly rural Virginia county located in the Piedmont section of the state with a population of twelve thousand, strikes it rich. The governor of Virginia, George Allen's slogan "Virginia Is Open for Business", has taken root.

The governor's office has informed Madison County officials that a Standard and Poor's Five Hundred company is looking for a location in Madison county to relocate its home office. Its requirement is one thousand and five hundred acres. One thousand acres would be used to build a state-of-the-art office complex, heliport, country club, an eighteen hole golf course, and houses for its employees. The remaining five hundred acres are to be used as a scenic buffer zone. A team of carefully chosen landscapers and architectures are now at work on planning this project. This will be a gate community completely enclosed with company employed security guards. A site in the southwest quadrant of Madison County is now being negotiated in the Hood area.

Of the two hundred families that will relocate to the county, ninety-six percent of their children are grown, in college, or go to private schools. No workload increase is anticipated for the sheriff's department. No additional Madison County tax dollars will be needed for road construction and improvements. Therefore it is estimated, at this time, that there will be a yearly excess surplus of three million dollars in Madison County tax income.

The governing body of the county is now contemplating several tax options. One is that land tax be deferred for all taxpayers presently paying taxes to the county. A second option is that all land taxes presently paid to the county could be used by the landowners to add additions and upgrade their homes, farm buildings, fences, etc., until the deferment is changed or revoked. The third option is that this surplus income would be invested in stocks or government bonds and used as needed.

State and county officials have invited its citizens to come forth with suggestions and comments, for they will receive their full attention.

April Fool

# Loose Mouth

Margaret Nicabacker was born into a third generation, wealthy, Boston shoe manufacturing family. She married young, and with a husband and three children, she decided to leave Boston and settle someplace in the South. She and Mr. Nicabacker searched the East coast from Maryland to the Florida border before deciding on a two hundred acres farm with a large house that had little character in a rural central Virginia county. Here she felt that she wouldn't have to fight the snow and cold and that she would be free of the Boston social scene.

She wasn't here long in her new home before she began to make her presence felt. She enrolled their two sons in the prestigious Woodberry Forest School, felt by many to be the most prestigious preparatory school in the South. And she then enrolled their daughter in the private secluded Foxcroft School, both in Virginia.

Among the possessions she brought to Virginia were hundreds of pieces of Tiffany silver and dozens of pieces of Lalique glass and Waterford crystal and early oil painting by listed artists. Also among the possessions were Queen Anne and Chippendale furniture of the best sort.

People in this rural county had never seen such large quantities of quality pieces in a home before. They were astonished.

Mr. And Mrs. Nicabacker named their farm Beacon Hill.

After Mrs. Nicabacker and her family were settled in and the children were away to school, she decided it was time for her and Mr. Nicabacker to entertain for now she felt that after Boston, entertaining here would be like a summer breeze. She frequently employed caterers from Washington, DC, and had her favorite caterer flown down from Boston to celebrate her and her husband's twenty-fifth wedding anniversary. Everyone who is anyone in the county was invited. Dinners and parties became regularly looked forward to events at Beacon Hill.

In the following several years she developed a reputation or perhaps it is better to say it surfaced, for being overly sensitive to any remarks that she thought were unfavorable to her and family, although she frequently said unkind things about others. Out of hearing range she was often referred to as Loose Mouth.

At one of her parties, she asked one of the male guests, who has a reputation for being a womanizer, if he were behaving of himself. He replied, "Hardly, what do you have in mind?" She rose from her chair as if she had sat on a pin, put her hands on her hips, and looked around the room to see who was amused. An immediate silence fell over the guests. It was as if Jesus had entered the room. The womanizer and his wife were never invited to Beacon Hill again.

As years passed, Mrs. Nicabacker had most of the elected officials as well as the influential people in her pocket. If the county governing body could not come up with all the cash needed to fund a project, she made up the difference. She did the same for charity drives. Some congregation members of her church now gave less because they knew that she would make up the difference.

Due to retirement age, the minister of her local church retired and was replaced by a young minister. Right away Mrs. Nicabacker clashed with the new minister, because he refused her request to condemn the right of a woman to have an abortion. When the church's governing body told the minister that Mrs. Nicabacker demanded that he be replaced, the minister said that Loose Mouth is at it again. He looked skyward and said, "Forgive me Lord."

Soon after Mrs. Nicabacker and her family moved to the country, she employed a local attorney by the name of Earl Stout to manage her large financial holdings.

Over the years the attorney siphoned small amount of her wealth. As time went by, he became more proficient and daring. Being a lawyer it was easy for him to learn how not to arouse suspicion and the countries that do not have extradition agreements with the United States.

He took a two weeks vacation to Santiago, Chile, and decided after making many contacts and gathering needed information that Chile would become his safe haven. Once back in the States, he began funneling money to his bank account that he established while in Santiago.

After he siphoned hundred of thousands of dollars from the Nicabacker family, he became aware that some people were becoming suspicious and asking alarming questions. He then bought and kept on his person for a quick getaway a one-way airline ticket to Santiago, Chile, from the Chile National Airline.

On the week before the authorities learned of his thievery, he made his move. He put all the cash he could muster into a carry-on bag and his other immediate needed belongings in a hold baggage suitcase. He departed Dulles Airport at 0900 hours on Chile National Airline flight 203 bound for Santiago.

He left behind a wife and two teenagers who knew absolutely nothing about his crime and desertion until the letter he posted at the airport was received by them. They never heard from him again.

At this time the Nicabacker family has learned everything and feeling their financial loss that their financial advisor and attorney has inflicted upon them.

A big city attorney who was hired by the Nicabacker's and the United States Customs official both informed them that without the cooperation of Chilean officials, there is nothing they can do.

Like Mrs. Nicabacker, their former financial advisor has the Chilean authorities in his pocket. Like the Nicabacker's, he can now live their life style, for the U. S. dollar goes much further in Chile than in America.

The Nicabacker's withdrew their children from private schools and enrolled them in the county public schools, and gave far fewer dinners and parties than before.

There are people in the county with a loose mouth but not the reputation who said that old Loose Mouth got what she deserved.

*J. Richard Grove*

# Well I'll Be Dog Gone

Big Dog and Little dog were mongrels who lived on the grounds between the White House, the Capital, and the Washington Monument. People were unfriendly and at best ignored them because they were mongrels and unkept.

One day while making their daily rounds past the White House grounds, a man on the inside of the fence spoke to them in a friendly voice. At first they were suspicious, but that person with the friendly voice surprised them again by speaking in an even lower and a friendlier voice. Big Dog and Little Dog came cautiously closer to the White House fence and poked their noses through the fence. The friendly voice on the other side came to the fence and patted both dogs on their heads. The two dogs were ecstatic with joy. Both did several complete turns and again put their noses through the fence. Again the friendly man patted both dogs on their heads. It was the President.

A White House gate policeman saw the President pat the dogs and told him as he walked past the White House gate that they were two mongrels and should be reported to the animal control officer. And that several times they have chased the dogs away from the entrance when they tried to enter the White House grounds.

As soon as the President returned to the Oval Office, he pressed the telephone button on his desk that gave him immediate access to the White House Chief of Security. The chief answered, "The chief here, Mister President." The President told the chief about his encounter with the two dogs and instructed him that it is his wish that everyone treat the dogs with kindness and that it is all right for them to enter the White House grounds.

Now when the President takes his daily walks, Big Dog and Little Dog always come to the White House fence to hear his kind voice and receive pats on their heads. When other people saw that the President was being friendly to the dogs, they now too became friendly to them. But Big Dog and Little Dog would not have anything to do with anyone but the President.

It wasn't long afterwards until Big Dog and Little Dog waited at the gate for the President so that they could join him on his daily White House grounds walks. After their walk with the President, both dogs would make a beeline for the gate because they still felt the gate police hostility to them.

Many months later as Big Dog and Little Dog were nearing the White House, they saw that

Pennsylvania Avenue was roped off and that many capital policemen were present. Both sides of the avenue were lined with people. As the dogs watched, even more people joined those that were already watching. People were five and six deep, even ten deep in places. As Big Dog and Little Dog were wondering, guessing, and watching at a distance, a large black vehicle drove through the main White House gate entrance and drove to the steps of the White House. Moments later eight high ranking military officers – two from each branch of the services – carried a long box-like object draped in the United States flag down the White House steps and slowly and carefully placed the coffin in the hearse.

Although Meow and Buster never accompanied the President on his walks, Big Dog and Little Dog knew they lived in the White House with the President and his family. Little Dog asked Big Dog if it were Meow. Big Dog didn't answer. Little Dog then asked if it were Buster. This time Big Dog answered that the box was too large for Buster – it must be the President.

As the hearse bearing the President's body proceeded up Pennsylvania Avenue toward the Capital, Big Dog and Little Dog followed. When they arrived at the Capital they saw that the Capital steps were roped off and that both sides of an open area going up the step were occupied by members of Congress.

Congressional members on the left side had mostly bowed heads and an exposed handkerchief was seen here and there. On the opposite side were congressional members of the opposition – several smiles could be seen and a light chatter was heard. A bottle cleverly concealed was being passed.

The President's coffin was removed from the hearse by the same eight military officers, who bore the body up on the Capital steps to lie in state.

Big Dog and Little Dog could not comprehend all that was taking place and the effect it would have on them. For several weeks they were seen daily at the White House gate entrance waiting for the President.

A big dog was found dead in the grass area across from the White House. A Washington newspaper ran an article on page three that the dead dog has been identified as Big Dog. According to this article and to people who knew the two dogs, it was believed that he died from a broken heart. Two days later Little Dog was found dead in the same spot the Big Dog was found.

# Mars Hall

In 1932, during the Great Depression, a Mr. Alfred Vanderbelt Hicks purchased a farm in Madison County, Virginia, located on the south slope of Allen Mountain. He purchased more adjoining land until he owned more than one thousand acres. During this same year, he and his family moved from New York City and Boston to the farm. Mr. and Mrs. Hicks came from privileged families where trust funds and ivy league education were the norm. The Hicks family was listed among the New York four hundred. It was not known in the county for years that they were socialites. They did not wear their Bond Brothers clothing, not even L.L. Bean, and did not drive foreign cars. They drove Chevys and Fords an did their shopping in local stores. They were fascinated with this new way of life and became fully engulfed. They both spent the rest of their lives here, seldom leaving the local area.

Mars Hall was an old country boy in his early twenties who grew up in the shadow of Allen Mountain and the nearby Conway River. Like other mountain folk of the time, he had only a couple years of schooling. Only country common sense was essential. Shortly after the Hicks moved to the country, Mars went to work for them.

There was a world of difference in the knowledge between the employer and the employee. Mr. Hicks never talked down to Mars, and when Mr. Hicks was in Mars's world, Mars never made Mr. Hicks look bad. Mars did not know the difference between an ascot and a cummerbund whereas Mr. Hicks did not know poisonous and nonpoisonous plants. In a sense they complemented each other. They always got along well together.

Mars still laughs when he tells of the day he took Mr. Hicks's fourteen-year-old son fishing in the Conway River. As they were crossing the cow pasture leading to the river, Mars scattered cowpies by a good swift kick. Alfred Jr. asked why he did this. Mars explained that if the cowpies were left alone, they would smother the grass and it would die; but if the cowpies were scattered, the grass benefited. The very next cowpie, the youngster thought he would give it a try. Wet cowpie flew in a hundred different directions. The city kid was wet with cow dung up to his waist. With no clothes on above the waist, he looked like he had suddenly came down with an unknown fungus attack. Mars forgot to tell Alfred Jr. that he kicks only the dry ones.

Mr. Hicks gets a sparkle in his eyes when he tells about all the pleasant moments he has experienced working with Mars over the years. One incident he recalls was that one year there was an exceptionally large amount of algae in the farm streams fed by springs. He asked Mars what all the green stuff was, and Mars answered, "Frog do." When Mr. Hicks told Mrs. Hicks that Mars calls salamanders spring keepers, she knew they did the right thing by settling in Virginia. "Mars," she said, "should have been a poet."

Mars knew the land and people as well as anyone. He knew who made the best moonshine and the best wines and brandies. During the holidays he had a yearly standing order from the Hicks to provide Christmas cheer for them and their friends. Mars had an over fondness for the bottle. Mr. Hicks was aware of this for quite frequently Mars did not come to work on Mondays. It reached a point where Mr. Hicks knew things could not continue this way, so he posted a sign in the farm shop that read – If you don't come to work on Monday, take the week off. After that, Mars never missed another Monday.

Mr. and Mrs. Hicks have passed on. Their son, Alfred, now lives on the farm in the big house with his family. Mars lives in one of the smaller farmhouses. He is now in his late eighties When he has had a good day and the weather is favorable, he will walk from the front porch to the back door. When he has had an exceptionally good day, he walks all the way around the house. He spends a lot of time on the front porch in his rocker. He knows his future is very limited, and he has prepared himself to meet his Maker.

Yesterday a hearse stopped at the big house and the attendant enquired where Mr. Hall's house was. Alfred cried for the first time since he as a boy.

The following day the mailman found the farm's mailboxes draped in black. He looked towards Mars's house and said, "Goody-bye old friend." As he was driving away, the lonesome call of a whippoorwill could be heard in the far distance.

# Madison County Sheriff

There is a new sheriff in Madison County. This dude is big, mean, ugly, and powerful. He stands seven feet one and tips the scales at three twenty. On each hip he packs a pearlhandle 38. He wears a rattlesnake hatband on his Stetson, which is the size of a sombrero. His cowboy boots are made from rattlesnake skins. Protruding from the top front of each boot is a rattler's head with fangs showing. Both pants legs are always tucked into his boots for maximum effect. His belt is also rattlesnake skin. The belt buckle is silver and the size of two open hands. Imposed on the buckle are thirteen small skull and bones. It is said that each represents justice – an unlucky, hardened criminal who ran out of luck. His great grandfather went west during the gold rush days and became sheriff of Sutter's Creek. Our sheriff now proudly wears his great grandfather's sheriff's badge. One day a brave Madisonian got up the nerve and very softly and politely informed the sheriff that the sheriff on his badge is short an "F." The sheriff gruffly told him that there ain't no need for a second "F." His nightstick looks like it might have at one time been a grubbing hoe handle.

The Board of Supervisors, the local governing body, voted to close the jail because, with the new sheriff in town, everyone with criminal intent is afraid to commit a crime. They now go outside of the county.

Seeing this dude walking down a street in Madison is awesome. Even though you may be law abiding, seeing him come toward you is frightening.

With the exception of small children and women, he calls everyone Rooster. Small children and women he calls Little Rooster; unusually pretty women he calls Ma'am.

After arriving home from grocery shopping at the General Store in Madison, my wife walks through our home calling "Richard!" She told me that she ran into the sheriff today and that he didn't call her Little Rooster – he called her Ma'am. He has since called a woman who lives in Criglersville Ma'am – and also a woman from Orange and one from Culpeper.

One of the old men sitting on the porch at the feed store wondered out loud why the sheriff calls only a few women Ma'am and all the others Little Rooster – what do these few have in common, he wondered.

After a few quiet moments another oldtimer spoke up and said that the SOB has an eye for pretty women. "Now you take that Gove woman who lives hear Hood, she is some kind of pretty, and those Criglersville and Orange and Culpeper women, they ain't mud fences."

The word has gotten out. Women come from far and wide to Madison, hoping to run into the sheriff. At bridge clubs, beauty shops, and places where women usually congregate, the talk is about the Madison County sheriff. They want to know if he will call them Little Rooster or Ma'am. Being called Ma'am by the sheriff now denotes status: class, beauty, and style.

If you ever visit Madison County and happen to run into the sheriff, you can be sure that he will ask "Where you from, Rooster?" My advice to you is to smile. Do not let your pride get you into a lot of unnecessary trouble, for it is far better to have hurt feelings than broken body parts. Dear visitor, no one kicks a dog that wags its tail.

Since this story was published in a local newspaper, things have been happening in Madison County. The sheriff is frequently asked the whereabouts of his pearlhandle 38's, rattlesnake boots and belt, and especially his belt buckle. Women have been seen to cross the street when they have seen the sheriff on the other side; and, in fun, they give him a big smile and a most pleasant greeting.

The high school students have picked up on the fun as well. The boys now call each other Rooster and, of course, the girls are Little Roosters. The boys call their girlfriends Ma'am.

One of the more daring boys called the principal Rooster. The principal hastily and firmly told the student that he was out of line and that he was to address him as "Mister" or "Principal." Several nearby students overheard the principal's remarks and now the students refer to the principal as Mr. Rooster.

Somehow the national media learned of these happenings in Madison County. Possibly a movie or possibly a television series will be made based on these happenings. Where will it end?

Madisonians, are you ready?

# Have a Good Day

Deep within the George Washington National Forest in the state of Virginia is the state's most favorite place for wild animals.

Like people, wild animals too have staked out areas where their kind have settled. Whether man learned this trait from animals or animals learned it from man, no one knows.

In this favorite place in the forest, known by all the animals as Kingdom, there is a section known as Possum Kingdom, and there is a Polecat Hollow and a Raccoon Ford and a Fox Ridge and a Groundhog Wallow.

Wild animals, again like people, have social systems. Polecats rank last and foxes are somebodies; within these groups, there is a difference. For instance, the more black a polecat is the higher he is thought of among his kind. Foxes, on the other hand, make no distinction according to color. Although red foxes may be somewhat favored over grey ones. It is their gait that determines their status. Those who do not drag their feet when walking and hold their heads high are the most respected. Raccoons are the bad boys of the forest. They are constantly getting into trouble – destroying bird nests, teasing and annoying babies of other animals, and destroying the peace with their rowdyism. Possums are just the opposite from raccoons. They just mozy along. Groundhogs are so busy digging burrows that no one really pays a great deal of attention to them.

For hundreds of years animals like birds have sought their own kind. But lately strange things have been happening in the Kingdom. First, a polecat was seen with a fox, and then two raccoons were seen with a possum. As time passed, it became common for all animals to socialize with one another.

Several miles north of Kingdom the government is constructing a power dam. During the groundhogs' cross-country trips, they discovered that the dam explosive foreman sometimes goes to sleep while on duty and neglects his duty even more by playing cards with his men. Of course the groundhogs couldn't resist exploring the shack where dynamite and dynamite caps are housed. It wasn't long before sticks of dynamite and dynamite caps were disappearing at an alarming rate. Groundhogs were carrying them back to Groundhog Wallow and stuffing them into their burrows. This went on for months. Soon the groundhogs had more explosives than the foreman. He never missed the explosives because he was so laid back and negligent in his duties.

One day there was a tremendous explosion in Groundhog Wallow, which is about centrally located in Kingdom, that approached the magnitude of a nuclear blast. All the animals outside of Kingdom heard the blast and some of these animals blamed the disappearance of Kingdom and the now unbelievable large hole on a Divine Hand for the wicked ways of those who lived there.

An old, wise, and very lucky groundhog who lived in Kingdom but was away at the time knew the real reason. He theorized that one of the young groundhogs who often played with explosives chewed on a dynamite cap and it exploded and this, in turn, ignited the thousands of sticks of dynamite.

All work on the government dam was stopped immediately; eventually the project was abandoned because all the steams in the watershed area of the dam now flowed underground. A hundreds of acres lake was formed in the area where Kingdom once was and is now fed by these underground steams.

Since this new, large lake is not shown on aeronautical charts, pilots flying over this area using visual flight rules sometimes become disoriented and must contact air traffic controllers for directions.

The old and wise groundhog places all the blame for the explosion on the dynamite foreman's negligence. He vowed that he would find the foreman and that he will somehow murder him.

If some day you are driving in the country and you see a groundhog alongside the road, do not think that he is waiting for you to pass so that he can cross the road safely. He wants to make eye contact with you, for he will never forget the eyes of the foreman.

If you are not the foreman, sing yourself a happy song and have a good day.

Ever since this story was written, many years ago, people have been using the expression HAVE A GOOD DAY.

# Poor Little Pig
## (written for boys and girls everywhere)

Poor Little Pig lived in the barnyard with all the barnyard animals. One day one of the barnyard animals stepped on Poor Little Pig's right front leg and broke it. Afterwards, he always walked with a limp. Poor Little Pig's tail didn't curl to the left or right as other pigs' tails do. It just hung down. Poor Little Pig was always so sad and lonely because all the barnyard animals always made fun of him.

One day the cow said to Poor Little Pig, "I don't like you because you are ugly and can't say moo." When the donkey heard the cow, he said, "I don't like you because you are stupid and can't say hehaw." The rooster said, "I don't like you because you are crosseyed and can't say cock-a-doodle-do." The sheep said, "I don't like you because your tail doesn't curl and you can't say baa." The horse said, "I don't like you either because you are a runt and can't say nay."

All of this was too much for Poor Little Pig. Poor Little Pig left the barnyard and wandered into the pasture and on into the woods. Poor Little Pig walked so far that he could not find his way back to the barnyard. Poor Little Pig was never seen again.

Days later the cow asked, "Where is Poor Little Pig?" The donkey said, "I don't know, but I miss Poor Little Pig." The rooster said, "I don't know, but I miss Poor Little Pig." The sheep said, "I miss Poor Little Pig." The horse said, "I don't know either, but I miss Poor Little Pig too."

Now that Poor Little Pig was gone forever, the barnyard animals knew that it was cruel and unkind of them for being cruel and unkind to someone so good and kind as Poor Little Pig.

Some day you will see a boy or girl who reminds you of Poor Little Pig. Do not be like the barnyard animals and wait until it is too late to show kindness.

# Something to Ponder

Just because a person has wealth and/or education is no assurance that that person has good taste.

Beware of a dog that does not wag its tail.

The smartest people are not necessarily those people who have PhD's from Yale, Harvard, Oxford, and other fine schools. The smartest people are those people who think the same things that you think.

It is dangerous to be alive.

Chevy bumper sticker: Friends don't let friends drive Fords.

Eternal Life is man's most beautiful dream.

Why all the concern about young people watching X-rated movies when they can watch the real thing on the Internet?

If there are people on this planet who do not have good common sense, they are not telling anyone.

You are not old until you have to sit down to put your pants on.

Bumper sticker: Don't be caught dead without Jesus.

If you don't need it, it isn't a bargain at any price.

Are pro-lifers willing to educate, clothe, and feed the unwanted children?

TV and computers are things that a bright young fellow dreamed up to keep old people from going batty from boredom.

Many African-Americans, including wealthy sports and entertaining figures, gravitate to crime as if crime were a black hole.

Bumper sticker: I love cats. They taste like chicken.

It is inhumane to deny terminally ill people the right to terminate their lives.

Confederate flag = red neck.

It is an undisputed fact that of all the criminals that have been put to death that not even one has committed another crime.

In order to preserve our countryside for future generations, why not draw an imaginary circle around all cities, towns, and villages and require all those who wish to build to build within these circles?

No one is as blind as those who do not want to see.

Should American continue to play Santa Claus and policeman to the world?

Do you miss soda fountains?

Women do a superb job of keeping their knees together and then they put on a skimpy bathing suit that reveals almost everything.

Why become the richest person in the cemetery?

In the days before the indoors toilet, country people would announce before going to the privy that they were going to see Mrs. Jones's daughter.

The older one grows, the easier it is to die.

If you want to see what the American wife wastes her family's dollars on, attend a yard sale.

On a recent trip to Europe, it was discovered that Americans are something that Europeans are not: FAT.

Today clothes no longer make the man; education does.

Those who do not doubt their own sexuality do not have a gays problem.

2000 years and still waiting?

Bumper sticker: This vehicle is insured by Smith and Wesson.

Do you think God really cares what you eat?

To solve presidential campaign financial problems, there should be a fund that anyone and money from any source could be contributed to. This fund would then be equally divided between qualified candidates.

Should working people who are not wealthy vote Republican or Democrat?

The European system for law suits should be adopted in America: The loser pays for both parties. This would eliminate frivolous law suits, and greatly reduce fattening lawyers pockets.

As sad as it may be, when industrialized nations and individuals provide life saving moneys to save children in third world countries, they are compounding the problem: For every child saved that child will produce a half dozen more children. These monies are misdirected to receive the maximum benefits – instead, these monies should be used for birth control and family planning.

Do you really believe that a human being lived for three days in a fish?

Although for the most part the contents of this book are fiction, it is my guess, if this book should somehow survive the next several centuries, those people living at this time will find many views in this book interesting.

If the Cuban people living in Cuba want to remain Communist, it is no one's business but theirs. And our government should commence normal relations with them.

Bumper sticker: Am I driving too closely?

# A Letter to Virginia's Governor Gilmore

Mars Hall
18167 Mars Hall Drive
Gordonsville, Virginia 22942
April 19, 2000

Governor James S. Gilmore, III
State Capital
P.O. Box 1475
Richmond, Virginia 23212

Sir:

Our Virginia Interstate Highways are extremely dangerous to travel on.

Recently I motored on I95 to and from Quantico from Fredericksburg and I81 to and from Roanoke from Harrisonburg. I maintained a constant speed of sixty-five miles per hour.

More than fifty tractor trailers passed me traveling from seventy to eighty-five miles per hour (my estimate). Are not our law enforcement officers and state officials aware that this is an invitation waiting for a massive pileup of vehicles and dead and mutilated bodies? Should not corrective action be taken now rather than wait until this happens?

A copy of this letter was sent to state senator Emily Couric.

Very truly yours,

J. Richard Grove

# ABOUT THE AUTHOR

The Author of *The Writings of an Old Virginia Country Boy* is an old Virginia country boy: he was born and grew up in the country—he picked apples, hoed and shocked corn, slopped and butchered hogs, milked cows, threshed grain, gathered eggs, and trampled through the fields and streams with a homemade fishing pole and a Sears Roebuck single shot .22 rifle—from preteens until Uncle Sam called during World War II.

After basic training, during which he could not understand why the soldiers were always complaining when all they had to do was walk while back on the farm he was used to grubbing with a mattock or swinging an ax, he was shipped to England during the war. This nineteen-year-old sargent was responsible for coordinating with U.S. Army commanders and British officials in moving U. S. troops and vehicles in and out of a designated area by road and rail in southern England.

After retiring from the military in 1965 and having seen Europe, country life and country ways called. A 340-acre beef cattle farm was the answer.

Today, after having lived for seventy-five years on this old planet and after having been to six continents and more than fifty countries, the lure of Virginia country life, country people, and country ways are as strong as ever.